Onwards and Upwards

Also by Cynthia Hallam and published by Ginninderra Press
*Bread and Butter People*
*Rising to the Occasion*
*Town Life*
*Living in the Moment*
*Moving with the Times*
*New Horizons*
*Here and Now*
*Life Happens*

Cynthia Hallam

# Onwards and Upwards

Heartfelt thanks to my daughter Trish for her ongoing encouragement and fearless editing, Warren Nicholls for keeping our writing group on track, Ben Farmer for his technical expertise, and Stephen Matthews OAM for his faith in my poetic endeavours.

Dedication
For Trish and Peter
Michael and Ben
with love always

*Onwards and Upwards*
ISBN 978 1 76109 441 5
Copyright © text Cynthia Hallam 2022
Cover image: Camila Esteves from Pexels

First published 2022 by
**GINNINDERRA PRESS**
PO Box 3461 Port Adelaide 5015
www.ginninderrapress.com.au

# Contents

| | |
|---|---:|
| Onwards and Upwards | 7 |
| Resolutions | 8 |
| Inheritance | 9 |
| Belonging | 10 |
| Just a Thought | 11 |
| Celebrity | 12 |
| The Bear Truth | 13 |
| A Bird's Eye View | 14 |
| Conscience | 15 |
| Bills! | 16 |
| Journeys | 17 |
| A Whale of a Time | 18 |
| Some Food For Thought | 19 |
| A Delicate Balance | 20 |
| A Seasonal Promise | 21 |
| Other People's Lives | 22 |
| Nursery Rhyming Timing | 23 |
| Communication | 24 |
| A Flight of Fancy | 25 |
| Obsessions | 26 |
| Instincts | 27 |
| The Test of Time | 28 |
| A Feline Perspective | 29 |
| Speed | 30 |
| Who's Aspirations? | 31 |
| Sprung! | 32 |
| The Fairy Tree | 33 |
| Forbearance | 34 |
| Kicking Up the Heels | 35 |
| An Interesting Life | 36 |

| | |
|---|---|
| A Matter of Opinion | 37 |
| The Covid Equation | 38 |
| And Life Goes On | 40 |
| Pie in the Sky | 41 |
| A Parking Lot Dissertation | 42 |
| Happenstance | 43 |
| Eat Your Heart Out, Mr Darcy! | 44 |
| An Unexpected Windfall | 45 |
| Chance | 46 |
| An Onion Autobiography | 47 |
| A Ticklish Situation | 48 |
| William's Confession | 49 |
| Beside the Sea | 50 |
| Punctuality | 51 |
| A Guilty Concession | 52 |
| The Excursion | 53 |
| A Puppy's Morning | 54 |
| Climate | 56 |
| Keira's Holiday | 57 |
| A Promising Career | 58 |
| Evolvement | 59 |
| Another Furry Tail | 60 |
| Interpretation | 61 |
| A Breakfast Table Conversation | 62 |

# Onwards and Upwards

This, and 'Sail thou forth to seek and find'
have been family mottos for generations
and by and large, have served us well
but sentiments have never been so valued
as in these current, uncertain times
when pondering the nature of the future
continually gets harder to envisage.

They strengthen us to uplift other spirits
with a compassionate understanding.
Inspire strong survival expectations
if we encounter unforeseen impediments
and engender a desire to move on.
Encourage attitudes of positive thinking
and searches for new possibilities.

## Resolutions

She decided the time had now come
to take a more positive outlook on life.
No more should'ves, could'ves or would'ves
that had been bruising her well-being
for more years than she cared to remember.
No more but what ifs on sleepless nights
weighing up the pros and cons
if some kind of decision was required,
then changing her mind at the last minute
when her embryo bravery faltered,
quite often to her ultimate disadvantage
when opportunities went begging,
so today, with a resolve firmly set in stone,
she booked her long, dreamed of cruise,
delighted with this first new arrangement.
After all, it wasn't on the *Titanic*, was it,
and *Ruby Princess* was such a pretty name.

# Inheritance

The screen door accidentally left ajar
is too much of a temptation for the tabby
who has been an indoor cat for years.
Cautiously she steps down onto the lawn,
pauses to feel its novelty
and with little experience of outdoor life,
is heading towards the busy road
when with uncanny timing,
she is spotted by the family Border collie.

Dormant sheepdog instincts kick in
as the feline's danger becomes apparent
and thinking they are playing a game,
she is innocently unaware
of being expertly herded towards home
until cornered at the steps,
followed nose to tail by her saviour,
she scampers up past their anxious mum
and the inadvertent exit route is closed.

Job now satisfactorily accomplished,
the canine superstar flops onto the floor
for a rewarding belly rub
and affectionate tickle behind the ears
then munches on a favourite treat.
Being a working dog sure had its merits!

# Belonging

'It can be no fun being old,' says Jim,
spreading his engaging, jovial smile
around the seniors who assemble
in the hall every Thursday morning,
'but it sure beats the alternative.'
Everyone nods and he continues on.
'We're here to encourage each other,
support each other and above all,
HAVE A GOOD TIME'
they all enthusiastically chorus.

A convivial morning tea is enjoyed,
rostered clearing up completed
and the scheduled Bingo proceeds
peppered with good-natured banter
until midday brings it to a close
and continuing to happily chatter,
hugging brief, cheerful goodbyes,
they all return home,
a comfortable feeling of belonging
still enfolding them in its arms.

# Just a Thought

The uncertainty of the weather is confounding.
One minute there is a glowing, benign sun
promising yet another salubrious day
and then it is overcast with incoming clouds
that even those clued-up gurus on the telly
had somehow, failed to elucidate,
despite reassuring charts and confident smiles.

But what if like pizza, we could just order it in?
A warm winter weekend for that barbecue
or a shower when the garden is starting to wilt.
Even a decent breeze for a harbour sail
or a sunny, windless day for our game of golf.

Only, what if others residing in the vicinity
are wanting something else at the same time?
Would a war break out between neighbours
or heated family infighting start flaring?
Could strangers reach any viable consensus?

So, with human character as quixotic as it is,
universal agreement is a utopian dream,
but at least, to the relief of us all,
we can put the blame onto Mother Nature
when our well laid plans are in disarray
and set about coping with any repercussions.
But gee! I wish I had brought an umbrella!

# Celebrity

Today, fame is such a transient thing.
Nobel Prize or Academy Award winners
barely get a fair share of accolades.
Pop star careers soar up to the heavens
until the public's attention is diverted
by another newcomer on the rise.
Even participants in those reality shows
enjoy some degree of prominence
before resuming their usual anonymity.

But although many icons from the past
will live on in our memories forever,
sadly, in an era of media saturation,
our notables are facing an uphill battle
to continue remaining relevant,
but those whose profiles are appearing
as clues in crossword puzzle books
know that at least their names
are still being drawn into the limelight.

# The Bear Truth

Well, we are off on another sleepless day.
The gates of our wildlife park are open
and the milling hordes will be pouring in,
tourist coaches full of strange people,
rampant, noisy schoolkids on excursions
and old-timers on a communal day out.

I'd much prefer to be home in the hills
but we were relocated after the bushfires
devoured our usual habitat, and I am still
getting used to this new way of living
but my favourite gum leaves are plentiful
so I do my best to show my gratitude.

But it seems we koalas are Aussie icons,
and crowds push in uncomfortably close
for a so called 'photo opportunity'
to record our brief, pointless encounter
but I AM trying to understand humans,
hoping they aren't always so unbearable.

# A Bird's Eye View

Now and then, when I am out in the yard
and the cockatoos are in raucous voice,
I ponder the nature of their communication.
Do their thought processes work like ours
and have an interest in each other's lives?
When they gather around the bird bath,
are they debating their next destination,
whether the peaches next door are better
or just passing the time voicing opinions
while they are taking some refreshment?

Perhaps discussing that great looking bird
they had encountered over in the park
or comparing the progress of fledglings
tucked safely away from predatory eyes
and how soon they will vacate the nest
to thankfully, start feeding themselves.
Maybe arguing over pecking order issues
or slamming my green, rotary clothes line
because the very peculiar looking tree
doesn't produce anything worth eating!

But my imagination is outreaching itself
so I think from now on, I will simply relax
and enjoy the ambience being created.

# Conscience

It always knows if you are naughty or nice.
Whether you stole a supermarket grape
and after tasting, didn't buy any.
Press avocados too hard to test ripeness
or drop one and just choose another.

Cross a road pretending not to have seen
a garrulous acquaintance is approaching
if you can't spare the time to chat.
Told a caller seeking yet another donation
that things are too tight at the moment.

If you drive into a car park the wrong way,
seeing a spot being vacated near the exit,
scoff a diet forbidden cream biscuit
or taken a few puffs of a covert cigarette
despite being praised for giving it up.

So when contrite thoughts are persisting,
all that we can do is trust our conscience
is so content with all our virtues
that in complaisance, turns a blind eye
to any minor, contemporary indiscretion.

## Bills!

No matter how economically savvy we may be,
or how clever at budgeting our resources,
we cannot stop the regular arrival of our bills,
all those insurances, power, water and rates,
the vet's bill for the new puppy's vaccinations,
all demanding our prompt attention,
but maybe to be really honest, it's just as well.

If there were no funds to provide the amenities
that every day, we all take for granted,
where would we be if there were no lights,
a driver without culpability ran into us
or our rubbish rotted uncollected at the kerb?
No power for winter warmth, summer relief
or to facilitate a consultation with Dr Google?

Like taxes, some will hurt us more than others
but as the well known adage wisely advises,
you can't have your cake and eat it too,
so we must accept these annoying impositions
as an integral element of civilised habitation
then suck it up, and enjoy a lifestyle
some nations would give anything to emulate.

# Journeys

There is a surprising plethora of journeying
that many of us undertake during our life,
from the simple day to day commuting
to the longest from childhood to maturity
then beyond into the fathomless unknown,
but along the way, we are experiencing
a medley of physical or emotional odysseys.

From depression to finding new inspiration,
those years discovering your true calling,
coping with an ongoing difficult situation
or voyages that only imagination ever take,
but one of the most favoured has to be
travelling with anticipation to loved ones,
who will be waiting to welcome you home.

# A Whale of a Time

On the night-time television news,
the annual migration of whales
from the Antarctic to warm waters
is a timely and welcome respite
from the endless restriction details
and growing complex of statistics.

These massive marine inhabitants
of our adjacent sea are as usual,
making the most of the pilgrimage,
frolicking in awesome displays,
unaware of their appeal to those
who don't have nature's freedom.

Sadly, the coverage is too fleeting
before switching to commercials
to have any therapeutic value
but can leave the viewers wishing
that we too could just take off
until things get back to our liking.

## Some Food For Thought

I feel sure that perennially iconic fish and chips
must be one of Australia's favourite foods.
Whether you fancy battered, crumbed or grilled,
the fish is always welcomed by your tastebuds,
hot chips, delightfully crunchy but soft inside,
much too often impossible to resist.

Whether breaking into the wrapping on a beach,
tucked up in a nice warm chalet at the snow,
crowded in a lounge room watching the footy
with your mates or just contentedly alone,
that familiar, comforting aroma will still linger on
in the recesses of our consciousness.

I guarantee, that if a random group was served
a masterpiece of exotic gourmet perfection,
some of the diners with unpretentious palates
would prefer to be assuaging their hunger
with much more mundane fish, chips and salad,
their appetites sighing with relief.

## A Delicate Balance

In our modern world, new technology
is transforming many young lives
and from observation, it appears that
their interaction seems to be waning.

Back in the day, before any devices,
they joined in family conversations
but can now opt for some gaming.
Chatting groups sauntered to school
developing enduring friendships,
entered learning curves of empathy,
but instead, during the regular treks,
heads can be down, fingers flying
and often, completely self-absorbed.

With internet a constant companion,
how will the young learn to handle
the complex relationships of real life?
I suppose they will just ask Google!

# A Seasonal Promise

While spring is still finding its feet,
my azaleas have jumped the gun again
and close to full, magnificent bloom.
In an early evening cinnamon glow
or under an azure morning sky,
those solid masses of pink blossoms
are an irresistible magnet for the eyes.
A banquet for the soul.

Casual clumps of unimposing freesias
are parading in the reflected glory,
confident that their perfume
is compensating for any lack of size
and while the lawn is dithering,
the rest of the garden is gearing up
to claim a fair share of our attention.
Reveal its full potential.

# Other People's Lives

In the car park of the mountain village shops,
a four-wheel drive and caravan attract attention,
each impressive in size and clearly up-market
as are the waterskis and kayak secured on top.

Perhaps someone famous is over in the café
having a mid-morning coffee break
while travelling west for an outback experience,
after a tour of our Aussie coastal delights.
Lucky lottery winners making the most of it
or a couple on a long-saved-for honeymoon
before settling down with a mortgage and kids.

An elderly woman with a shopping bag arrives,
briskly unlocks the driver's side door
and settles comfortably behind the wheel.
She expertly manoeuvres the cumbersome rig
through the exit into the highway traffic,
Range Rover and driver firing on all cylinders,
leaving the dumfounded locals still wondering.

# Nursery Rhyming Timing

The verses for children are still around
but today, several are rather inappropriate.

Georgie would be expelled from school
for kissing those girls and making them cry.
Single mothers with too many children
live in social housing instead of shoes
but the fact that she had thrashed the kids
before sending them famished to bed
would have protection authorities seething.

Humpty might well have survived his fall
had a modern ambo come to his aid.
If the tails of disabled mice were cut off,
animal activists would raise the roof.
Delusional people still claim to be teapots,
but possibly under the influence of ice.

We now understand why stars twinkle,
psychologists can sort Mary's contrariness,
give Miss Muffet arachnophobia therapy,
but heaven forbid labelling sheep black!
       So Fee Fi Fo Fum,
          the jury's still out on that one.

## Communication

Deeply absorbed in his phone,
a youth is leaning against the wall
outside the shopping centre doors,
and with resigned obedience,
a huge shaggy dog sits beside him,
so animal lover that I am,
I cannot resist a smiling 'Hello'
and to my total surprise
it returns a hairy, canine grin
and enthusiastically wagging tail,
my day completely uplifted
by the delightful, brief encounter.

# A Flight of Fancy

For weeks, she has enjoyed its presence
and as usual, from nowhere it has arrived,
hovering while she hangs out the clothes.
Other days it settles nearby as she hoses,
prunes the shrubs or pulls the weeds.
Regardless of the time, it emerges on cue
whenever she sets a foot into the yard.

According to other people in the street,
whenever she mentions these encounters
it's just an annoying, cabbage moth pest
but to her it remains a dear little butterfly
that seems to enjoy her company too
for after she says hello it flutters its wings
just that little bit faster she truly believes.

Once, she worried that she may be known
as that batty old lady who talks to herself
but to be honest, she no longer cares
as once again, to her enormous pleasure,
it escorts her back towards the house,
but forever free in its own natural habitat,
has no clue why she toils so often in hers.

## Obsessions

Ted had only two real interests in life,
greyhounds Bonny Lad and Bonny Lass
who were his sole reason for living.
Bonny Lass's recent form was promising
and Bonny Lad had almost won a race
but unfortunately, when overtaking
the alluring Sahara Sally he lost his focus
and sired a highly unwelcome litter.

Vera had a consuming preoccupation,
her Siamese cats, Princess and Contessa
who were the focus of her existence,
and like Ted, loved regaling their virtues
to people in the neighbourhood.
She knew a lot about the feline world
and didn't hold back on her knowledge
when she ran into some company.

So it a was quite a relief to everyone
when Ted and Vera eventually met,
each delighted to have found someone
who'd patiently listen until their turn
to report the latest four-footed activity,
but possibly, the only one thinking
of anything of a more personal nature
may be happy-go-lucky Bonny Lad.

# Instincts

Tim had never been known for quick thinking,
but when the child skips onto the highway
and a semi, brakes screaming, unable to stop,
he launches himself into the closing gap,
grabs a firm hold of the frightened little girl
and makes a heroic backward leap to the kerb.

As the laden truck halts barely metres ahead,
the mother arrives to comfort her child,
then, turning to Tim, sprawled in the gutter,
chastises him for bruising her daughter's arm.

As he watches them return to the park gates
with no further interest or interaction,
he feels guilty for what he must have done,
his own arms bleeding, a shoulder on fire,
as the driver and bystanders rush to his aid,
human compassion, still alive and kicking.

## The Test of Time

Braving the crush of Saturday shoppers,
an elderly couple stroll around the mall,
hand in hand in lively conversation.
They pause at a furniture shop's display,
an item having caught their attention
and is now fuelling their intimate smiles.

Also holding hands, another pair arrive,
the eager young woman heading inside,
but soon, an altercation is brewing,
engagement ring glinting as she points,
but he just keeps shaking his head
and impatience bristling, moves her on.

The veteran duo saunter off, deciding
to come back later after some thought,
but the others keep on bickering
and with both still stubbornly at odds,
their relationship clearly in distress,
should also take time to think it over.

# A Feline Perspective

In the past, it has never been discussed,
but dogs have always been overrated.
They can't even take care of themselves
and that's where we cats are superior.

Canine personal hygiene is non existent,
leaving excrement wherever they are
instead of hiding it in a private location.
Our bathing is constant and by choice,
but dogs depend on human inclination.

They revel in a patronising 'Good dog!'
after doing anything remotely clever.
Are forced to endure tethered 'walkies'
so they and their boss get to exercise,
but WE practise our own fitness regime
as we are leaping, chasing or climbing,
being by nature, so much more athletic.

To be fair, working dogs are exceptions.
At least, they can be out saving lives,
sniffing for drugs or rounding up sheep
while we are exterminating rodents,
but overall, in evaluating the equation
we deserve by far, the most respect,
so with no personal bias I rest my case.
(And if I say so myself, 'Good cat!')

# Speed

It is Sunday afternoon, and at a lightning pace,
the motorbike is roaring back and forth
along the usually tranquil suburban street,
youthful rider oblivious to residents emerging
to ascertain the cause of the disturbance,
but when aware of the attention he is receiving,
he continues with his deafening escapade,
whooping and waving until suddenly all is quiet.
Apparently, he has run out of fuel
and needing all his strength to retain mobility,
he trundles the bike past his neighbours
who grinning, resume their weekend activities
as ruefully, he copes with his embarrassment.

# Who's Aspirations?

As usual, when Damien scored a leading role
in his school's annual drama production,
his mum treated him so much like a superstar
she had her only child believing it himself.
After the show, he remained waiting around
in case anyone wanted his autograph
until too embarrassed by his silly posturing,
his mates vanished, laughing behind his back.

When he revealed his loneliness to his mum,
she patted his arm and said not to worry.
That when he was famous all over the world,
they'd brag they went to school with him,
but retiring to his room to do some thinking
with his loyal canine companion by his side,
he realised that his recent behaviour
had blinded him to the reality of his future.

Watching a favourite episode of Country Vet
confirmed his passion for the animal world
and resolved that this was the profession
where in fact, his authentic ambition lay.
So now, tending his first four-footed patient
he smiles, recalling that life changing day,
his pleasure vindicating the crucial decision,
but his mum still needed some convincing.

# Sprung!

Spotlit by a ray of golden, early morning sun,
a cockatoo perches on top of the rotary line,
part-eaten lemon grasped firmly in a claw
and with full concentration keeps on pecking
at its all-engrossing, pilfered refreshment.
Evidenced by copious detritus under the tree,
the others have abandoned the covert foray
but this one seems oblivious to its disclosure.

The local possums have always been blamed
for the annual decimation of the citrus crop
due to the nocturnal nature of their lives
so with evidence now staring me in the face,
I feel guilty for my erroneous assumption.

It wouldn't be so bad if they devoured them,
but obviously, after nibbling under the peel
have found the contents a bit distasteful,
dropped the remainder onto to the grass
then tried another, another and yet another.

True to form, the cocky reacts as expected,
repast tossed away with a derisive squawk
before leaving to join the rest of its gang,
sleeping off their successful overnight raid.
So if any possums know of my accusations
I assure them, my apology is still sincere,
but, I don't think cockies are night flyers
so just a modicum of doubt is still lingering.

# The Fairy Tree

Kerbside, further down our street
a tree with dense low branches
has enlivened the neighbourhood
for as long as I can remember.
Someone with a rich sense of fun
nailed a tiny door to the trunk,
and ever since, items of fairy life
have interchanged, as passers-by
are attracted by the fantasy
and cannot help getting involved.

The offerings are an eclectic mix,
a whimsical collection of all kinds
of diminutive paraphernalia,
cocktail umbrellas, a mini swing,
ceramic toadstools, tinkling bells
and even a little clothes line
ready for gossamer pixie apparel.

But, even though the existence
of these fanciful fellow residents
stays firmly in the imagination,
a new, delicately painted sign
avowing 'Butterflies Welcome'
and branches strewn with glitter
can still have you wondering
if anyone has recently moved in.

# Forbearance

In the waiting room of the medical centre,
the toddler, who is sitting beside his mother,
is expertly manipulating a mobile phone,
completely absorbed in his eager exploration
until a receptionist signals her appointment.

His mother rises and reaches for the device
but her child, loudly protests the interruption
and has a dummy spit of epic proportions.
The ongoing tug-of-war attracts all attention
as vehemently, he refuses to hand it over.

Her embarrassment and frustration escalate,
and with his tantrum in full, aggrieved fury,
they are ushered to the family doctor's door,
who, yearning for the earplugs in his desk,
digs deep for his usual professional decorum.

# Kicking Up the Heels

The town's Seniors Club social is in full swing
and when the supper dance is announced,
Clive approaches Stella full of confidence.
'Come on,' he booms, pulls her to her feet
and finds herself enfolded in a firm embrace
then plunged right into the passing throng.

He smiles, unaware of her apprehension,
'Hear you were a hoofer in the old days,'
he bellows while barrelling his way around,
oblivious to the other dancers on the floor,
'Well, I was once a chorus girl at the Tivoli,'
she manages while evading his boots,
appalled as they jostle yet another couple,
but unable to easily disengage his grip,
continues to be vigorously propelled along.

As thankfully, the music comes to an end,
she asks him what he did before retiring.
'Drove a bulldozer for the council,' he says,
which explains it all in Stella's estimation
and after a brief rub of her affronted shins,
they head for some convivial refreshment.

## An Interesting Life

Harry had led an adventurous, lucky life.
Misfortune seems to have befallen him
all over the world yet he still survived.
Once he was miraculously rescued
when an Austrian bend was misjudged
and they teetered over a precipice
before being saved by the coach behind
as his own slipped out of securement.

In Africa he was savaged by a wild boar,
and treated by a doctor on the tour
who prevented him from bleeding out.
A Tibetan landslide nearly claimed him
but a single tree provided refuge.
In Cuba, a bullet just missed his jeep.

But back at home he tripped on a step,
falling down onto the concrete below,
and Lady Luck abandoned him,
so now he is off on another journey,
no doubt, planning tours through
the hereafter's famous Elysian plains,
life's misadventures just a memory.

# A Matter of Opinion

The cold snap has caught us all by surprise.
Lulled by a pleasant and temperate summer
and until now, a surprisingly warm autumn,
the icy blast sweeping up from the Antarctic
has us digging out the blankets and fleeces
with considerably more urgency than usual.

In town, even the local pigeons are in shock.
Feathers fully fluffed, huddled on the grass
in a patch of sun, they are abnormally quiet
and even the crumbs dropped by someone
eating a pie in the bus stop shelter nearby
haven't tempted any of their usual interest.

A shirt-sleeved Tradie is unloading his ute
and assures us passing shivering shoppers
'The cold is just all in your mind, you know,'
but I think that later on, after I get home,
I'll be putting on the heater and settling in,
pigeon wisdom deemed the more reliable.

# The Covid Equation

Haltingly, our lives are moving forward
yet only about twelve months ago,
who could have envisaged that a virus
would still hold citizens to ransom
and living not returned to the familiar.
That an evolving disease would impact
the wellbeing of so many in our nation.

On again off again restrictions remain
disrupting our days with regularity,
like where and when to wear a mask
and the instant closure of borders
leaving business and family interaction
in disarray and you can't help wonder
if this is a portent of future 'normal'.

But being regarded as a lucky country,
a positive counter balance is evident.
Families enjoying more together time,
cycling out and about on weekends.
Young people finding to their surprise
that playing board games can be fun.
Cheaper than nights out on the town.

The joy of owning a pet is growing
as dog walking is filling spare time.
Our cupboards are tidier than ever,
charity shops reaping the benefit.
Mask wearing is alerting offenders
with bad breath to take action,
preventing more embarrassment.

The inland is embracing travellers
holidaying here and not overseas,
igniting signs of local recovery
after the drought, floods and fires.
Even the caravan industry thrives.
Hand washing is more prevalent
so the flu has been less passed on.

So basically, it comes down to this.
Life, like toilet paper, can't recycle,
so maybe we should value more
the freedoms we take for granted.
Cope with the inconveniences,
make our own existence worthy,
ever thankful to live down under.

## And Life Goes On

Sunday morning on an early winter's day
and our town is bristling with activity.
The car park nearly full, supermarket busy
but the usual queuing up at the checkout
much more relaxed than on a week day
with all its other pressing considerations.

The coffee shops and cafes are crowded
while at tables on the footpath outside,
groups are deep into lively conversation,
canine companions asleep at their feet
after a few slurps from water bowls
the proprietors provide for their benefit.

How lucky we are to live in a community
that cares about the welfare of others.
Not too small for up-to-date amenities
or too big to lose the sense of belonging.
In fact, as far as any comparisons go,
just right, according to us biased locals.

# Pie in the Sky

Katherine is watching a cooking show
where the well-known chef and judge
is applying flames to the top of a tart
and being a mediocre cook she sighs,
knowing if she tried the delicate task
it would turn out a blackened disaster,
her fingers burned, her apron on fire
and the pie plate in danger of collapse.

She dreams of baking a culinary treat
and after declaring a modest, 'Ta dah,'
serving it up to her admiring guests
but likelihood simply wishful thinking.
On other channels, owners renovate
houses in better condition than hers
but she can't hammer a straight nail.
Singing competitions are a lost cause,
just a lot of noise to tone-deaf ears.

So, unable to locate another interest,
the usual garden program is a refuge,
her dwindling morale again uplifted
by a fortunate, inherent green thumb
and spurred by horticultural viewing,
she decides to resume her ambition
to invent, a remote-controlled rake,
and rendering a 'Ta dah' with pride.

# A Parking Lot Dissertation

I wonder if anyone else has noticed
that the shopping centre's parking
is a microcosm of human behaviour?
The selfish straddle of defining lines
changing two scarce spaces to one.
Queue jumpers with no conscience,
trolleys dumped and not returned,
or the person suddenly reversing
out of a park, to fix a bad alignment
and you brake to a juddering halt,
or end up sideswiped by someone
who didn't bother to check behind.

Yet the outlook isn't just negative.
There's the teenager who runs after
a runaway trolley as a Mum juggles
a toddler, baby and her shopping.
The staffer carrying a senior's bags
and unloading them into her car.
The kind driver on the road outside,
slowing down traffic to let you out.

But oops! My thoughts elsewhere,
I did not notice her open her boot
then step back in contemplation.
Phew! All good with no harm done
but both of us verifying my theory.

# Happenstance

After realising she should be socialising more,
Julie had decided to attend a singles dinner
at the newly opened club in a suburb nearby,
but it is not turning out the way she imagined.
On the one hand, the meal selection is great,
nice music providing a congenial atmosphere
but her table mates leaving a lot to be desired.

On one side, the bloke wolfing down his meal
is totally uninterested in polite conversation.
On the other, the fellow is so full of himself
that his self-promoting has spoilt her appetite.
The woman opposite just glares at everyone
so she feels that getting away is imperative,
writing off the evening as a complete disaster.

Seated outside, a man is cradling a backpack
and asked if he is going in, he shakes his head
then she recognises his probable situation,
so regardless of her decision goes back inside,
re-emerging with a hot pie, chips and coffee,
his grateful smile warming up her very soul,
the dismal outing now an unexpected delight.

## Eat Your Heart Out, Mr Darcy!

He was undeniably, very handsome
and seemed happy they had met,
so, sinking into lonely spinsterhood,
she was glad that she could recall
her instinctive, culinary expertise
for he was now the beneficiary
and the hospitality she had on offer
encouraging a growing interest.

As they spent more time together,
content with each other's company,
she knew it was a perfect match.
Not only was he a genial presence
but bringing joy into her daily life
so it was a no-brainer to conclude
the stray tabby had a forever home
and both blessed with salvation.

## An Unexpected Windfall

Leaving a favourite author's novel,
she gathers her mail from the box
including a gaudy, heavy envelope,
ignoring it as just more marketing,
but intrigued by its unusual bulk,
finds only the expected catalogue.
Then a scratchy falls into her hand
and discovers that if she can reveal
two matching squares on the grid,
she could win ten thousand dollars
so thinking why not, she has a go,
and incredibly, two are the same.
Her longed-for holiday is a reality!

Heart racing, she prepares to claim,
aghast at what she nearly missed
but first she must make a purchase,
and selects some unwanted item,
for even with a hefty postal charge,
worth it for her dream to happen.
Her euphoria happily simmering,
she continues filling in the form
but discovers is only 'in the draw'
for the prize, no time frame given,
so crushing it, reopens her book
to assuage her disappointment.
Renew her faith in happy endings.

# Chance

When suddenly, opportunity knocks,
we face an immediate dilemma.
Our present life's fabric may change,
and in a flash, must be considered
in case it impacts on our well-being.

Will it live up to what we really want?
Being offered that fantastic job
is wonderful, but will the commute
spoil our present work/life balance?
Leave us to regret our impetuosity?

Would a chance opportunity to buy
at a ridiculously low price be a coup
or turn out to be just another scam?
Is the unscheduled interruption
worth dividing our vital attention?

Captains of industry and the forces
make these judgements every day
often with worldwide implications,
unlike the rest of us mortals
with most problems self-relevant.

But correct, instinctive response
would be a valuable talent to have,
and lectures should be on offer
but alas, those who'd most benefit
are the ones least likely to enrol.

# An Onion Autobiography

It is a paradox having my credentials.
On one hand, I am welcomed
yet on the other can engender tears,
so with mixed feelings I bare my soul.
Give an insight into my life.

My progress to maturity was earthy
then unique qualities displayed.
Was acquired by someone with taste
and respectfully disrobed, revealing
my true, inner personality.

Sharing a pan with pumpkin is okay,
for its colour compliments mine,
but I deplore these insipid potatoes,
yet their company is very warming
so one tries to be tolerant.

Oh! I'm being lifted to be admired,
mouth open, utterly stunned,
so I am eager to see what follows.
Trust sharing this new experience
will leave my dignity intact.

# A Ticklish Situation

'I need to get something off my chest,'
says Steve, looking uncomfortable.
He and Jen are having an alfresco meal
in their backyard and she stops eating,
concerned by the growing uneasiness
she has been observing for some time.

What is making her darling husband
so distracted and squirming in his seat?
Scenarios of calamity come to mind.
Is he having an affair with a workmate
and is wanting to move in together?
Are the mortgage payments in arrears
owing to some hidden gaming debt?
Has he damaged her prized new car?

Then he stands and yanks off his shirt,
venting a fervent cry of anticipation.
'Got the bugger,' he yells in triumph
and brushes the ant onto the lawn
puts his T-shirt back on, smiles at Jen
and turns his attention to his steak.

# William's Confession

Mind you, he was always very pleasant
but you generally got the impression
that Kevin wasn't playing with a full deck
if you know what I mean,
so when my old neighbour wandered in
as usual to see what I was doing,
I just continued to tidy up the garage.
When I came upon the dusty little picture,
I admit that with a tad of condescension
I said, 'Pretty,' as if I was showing
a fairy tale illustration to some toddler.

Kevin looked at it closely, reached for it
and replied, 'It's very nice. Can I buy it?'
'Sure. Twenty quid,' I said to humour him.
and to my surprise, he took me seriously,
pulled out his wallet and handed it over.
Well, if it made his day, why not?
But I read in the paper the following week
of the early Aussie masterpiece found
for which a gallery paid a generous sum,
and under, a smiling photo of Kevin,
his hand of cards definitely a royal flush!

## Beside the Sea

It is an early winter's morning at the beach,
yet groups of people are relaxing along the sand.
I can smell the ozone on the incoming breeze,
taste the salty tang on my tongue from the surf
where hardy souls are ignoring the chill
and making the most of today's sunny weather.

Two seagulls are competing for a potato chip
held out by a grinning teen until there is a victor
then shrugging, offers his last one to the other,
and impressed by the innate compassion,
I am reassured that the upcoming generation
will carry our worthwhile values into the future.

# Punctuality

Being on time had been a credo in her family
for many generations.
Better half-an-hour early than five minutes late
asserted the familiar mantra of her youth
and never given it any real thought,
but been automatically complying all her life.
On social occasions,
family members would always turn up early
so slyly, hosts would advise a later time
that would better suit their arrangements.

Then recently, one of the newest generation
would roll up late to family gatherings
to much tut tutting and general disapproval
but to her surprise,
the roof didn't fall in or world stop turning
so she realised, that perhaps,
she was unconsciously locked into a rigidity
that while laudable, didn't suit everyone
and welcomed this fresh outlook
to reassess her own self-imposed behaviour.

# A Guilty Concession

Along the supermarket aisle,
an elderly woman hobbles behind a trolley,
her left foot encased in plaster,
and Bernice voices sincere commiserations
for her unfortunate accident
but she says, 'No, I was actually really lucky,
for I can still drive my car with my right,'
and throws another bar of chocolate
into a trolley already containing a selection
of potato crisps, biscuits and soft drinks.

'I fell off a ladder,' she adds,
'hanging new curtains in my bedroom,'
as confidently she continues her purchasing
and suddenly, it occurs to Bernice
that maybe, living a long and healthy life
might not always rely on exercise and salad
so drops a packet of cream biscuits
onto her lettuce, carrots and low-fat milk
before hurrying over to the checkout,
then aerobics class to ease her conscience.

# The Excursion

'Fasten your seat belts, ladies and gentlemen.
This may be a rather bumpy ride,' says the driver.
'I was on a bit of a bender last night
so my reflexes might be slightly off the mark
but there's no need to worry,' he continues,
'I'm used to driving these tricky mountain roads
so I should be able to cope with them today.'

There is dead silence in his coachload of seniors
and he realises his welcoming jest has misfired,
that his passengers are feeling uneasy,
so quickly adds a bold wink and a broad smile
until everyone relaxes and starts to laugh,
ruefully drops the microphone back into place
and smoothly eases into the highway traffic.

# A Puppy's Morning

The man is off to work and she's taken the kids to school
so I've got the whole house to myself at the moment
except for that dreadful old fleabag they call Natasha.
I've had breakfast and there is a bowl of Puppybites
in case I get peckish and need to have an extra snack.
The cat has lived here longer than me and she is jealous
but I think that she really quite likes me and why not?
I'm so easy to love, aren't I?

She's asleep on the lounge, tail hanging over the edge,
so I think I might give it a little nip to wake her up
to see if she wants to play, but she's swiped at my nose
and now scratching her post glaring at me all the time
so I'll just go into the girl's room and get her teddy
to have a bit of a game then leave it behind the curtain
to give them all heaps of fun, trying to find her bear
when she is ready for bed.

Right. Now into the kitchen to have a bit of a nibble,
but oops, I've knocked the water bowl onto my snacks
and most of them have washed under the fridge
with only a few left in a puddle, but while eating them
I've got lots of wet, smelly mush all over my feet
so I'll go into the lounge room and wipe it off in there
because I'm not allowed to jump up on the cushions
so I will not get the blame.

Now, why is Natasha heading towards the front door?
Ah. A car is coming up the drive so I'll hop into bed
and pretend to be asleep when the lady comes in
then SHE will get yelled at for the messy kitchen floor
and stop her carrying on with all that purring stuff.
Yep, this's what a smart pup would do in this situation.
I mean, you can't always rely on being this gorgeous
every single time, can you?

# Climate

Generally, we are summer or winter people
and this does not follow family traits.
Each individual finds pleasure or displeasure
in whatever the annual rotation offers.

Some love winter's atmosphere of cosy fires,
fingers wrapping around hot drinks.
Skiers love hurtling down the snowy slopes,
all that socialising inside of an evening.
Those satisfying thick soups and solid meals
and fresh tingle when venturing outside.
The fact that body shape is of no concern
being well camouflaged by woollies.

Yet others delight in the welcome freedom
that summer's weather can provide.
Longer days, outdoor games and activities,
swimming, kayaking and barbecues
and wait impatiently for warmer weather
to abandon the extra layers of clothes
and weighty pile of blankets on the bed.
Farewell all those frosty mornings.

But Mother Nature uses her own calendar
so we must cope and get on with life,
whoever we are or wherever our location
despite any personal idiosyncrasies.

# Keira's Holiday

Entering the boarding kennel foyer
with Keira, their Border collie,
she realises that a very similar dog
is seated by someone's feet,
and she immediately senses that
a frisson is building between them.
Briefly, they size each other up
then sniffing, make an approach,
and after a prolonged nuzzle,
they roll over in a mutual embrace,
whimpering in ecstasy
as an old connection is rekindled.

A chat with the other dog's owner
reveals that the pair of them
were litter mates seven years ago,
and delighted by the coincidence,
make everyone else aware,
so they are housed, eat and frolic
in a relaxed, joyful atmosphere
of companionship for a week,
until their unforseen reunion ends
when it is time for Keira to leave
and is driven back home,
comforted by her forever family.

# A Promising Career

With you all the way, says the aspiring politician
to the disadvantaged group of city residents
then steps back into his Mercedes to have lunch
at the poshest restaurant in the area.

With you all the way, he declares with passion
in a speech warning against global warming
before leaving in his private plane for a break
at his family's island holiday resort.

With you all the way he says to island residents
concerned about their gradual taking over
by foreign interests, before flying back home
to accept his own, lucrative offer.

With you all the way, he greets when arriving
half way through his local branch meeting,
unaware, voting for the new representative
is now over and that he has lost.

With you all the way he proclaims once again
to the gathering, shaking people's hands,
wrongly assuming that the nomination is his,
but this time, no one is listening.

# Evolvement

Time moves on in perpetual motion
regardless of other considerations,
relentless in its steady advance
and totally in control of our planet,
the one constant in a volatile world.
Night and day, every living thing
is affected by a need to encompass
the outcomes of its progression,
and evolving to consolidate survival,
as constant, transient conditions
impact on our day to day well-being.
Make us what we have become,
regardless of our own intentions.

From a purely human perspective,
our inherent creative inclination
has diversified our overall thinking.
Instant communication rules
and business success the holy grail,
but worthy endeavours multiply.
Countries helped out of adversity.
Life other than ours respected.
We are now living a little longer
due to the landmark innovations
with a genesis back in the day,
confident of tomorrow's arrival
and an unfolding, positive future.

## Another Furry Tail

Shadow has been truly well named.
This enormous cat's fur
is a very attractive shade of grey,
an imposing set of lengthy whiskers
enhancing his air of distinction.

When his housekeeper has visitors,
he rises from his slumber
to accompany them on the tours
of home and garden improvement,
his presence taken for granted.

He has a natural, dignified manner
that radiates confidence,
makes her friends feel privileged
that he was there, escorting them
on inspections of his domain.

But as his minder lives on her own,
he is a great companion
so she enjoys taking care of him,
board and lodging entirely repaid
by his gift of total devotion.

# Interpretation

The timelines on our groceries are confusing,
difference in a 'use by' and 'best before'
open to the discernment of the buyer.

A 'use by' is quite emphatic in its meaning
but 'best before' has implications.
Does it mean that for an indefinite time
won't poison us or taste like rubbish?
It causes angst when a cupboard search
locates a required, rarely used ingredient
then realise it had been there for years,
quite possibly two Christmases ago,
but not registered a need for replacement.
Have suppliers added a dodgy ingredient
and precluded any repercussions?
Producers not bothered to check viability
and unable to be any more specific?

I guess we must trust our own perceptions.
Just another decision while out shopping.
Extra stress we could well do without.

# A Breakfast Table Conversation

Ah. At last. This is feeling more comfortable.
For an eggcup, you are being so compassionate
and refreshing after all that boiling water.

Thanks. Sorry you've had no time to cool down
but as usual, the kid is late for school
and now he's scraping your yolk all over me
so thank heavens you are rather overcooked.

Well, it is not my fault that he's a sloppy eater.
Think about what befell a mate of mine.
One minute he's happily cocooned in a carton
and next, because of someone's allergy,
spread disgustingly all over a bathroom floor!

Yeuch! At least I'm surviving his spoon today.
Yesterday, he very nearly chipped my rim.

Oh stop whingeing and look what's happened.
He has left some of me behind in my shell
and his mother is definitely none too pleased.

But I am. I love feeling your body next to mine
and to be honest, I am really getting off on it.

Aw. I'll bet that you say that to all the eggs.

Well perceived, my dear. That is quite possible.

www.ingramcontent.com/pod-product-compliance
Lightning Source LLC
Chambersburg PA
CBHW070337120526
44590CB00017B/2925